DONALD TRUMP
A POLITICAL TUMULT

MARIO CHATEAU

This election is one for the books.

DONALD TRUMP
A POLITICAL TUMULT

MARIO CHATEAU

ISBN 978-0-9967528-0-0

mrjchateau@yahoo.com

DONALD TRUMP
A POLITICAL TUMULT

MARIO CHATEAU

Contrary to popular beliefs that you should study political science to run for office, you would be surprised to see an individual with no political knowledge but a populist message draws big crowd.

Mario Chateau

People always choose a leader that they can identify with.

POPULISM

In the past few years, the United States government was among the superpowers that have fought populist's ideologies in so many regions around the world. They were afraid of the message of change and hope that those populist leaders carried out to their people – messages that contradicted often with their political interests.

Mario Chateau

I n the 1980s, a movement best-known as theology of liberation - viewed as socialist by many conservative clerics - has developed within the Catholic Church in Latin America.

That movement met opposition in the United States that accused it of using 'Marxist Concepts.'

Perceived as a religion of the poor because it emphasizes liberation from social, political, and economic oppression as an anticipation of ultimate salvation, conservatives scorned it as overly Marxist and the Vatican treated it with hostility.

Grown into an international movement that has been controversial in the Catholic theological community and condemned by Pope John Paul II and Pope Benedict XVI, the rise of the liberation theology has challenged alliances between church and state; and some radical priests called for social, political and economic change.

Archbishop Oscar Arnulfo Romero - who was a conservative and later adhered to that movement due to unfortunate circumstances - said on March 11, 1979: "When the church hears the cry of the oppressed it cannot but denounce the social structures that give rise to and perpetuate the misery from which the cry arises."

Romero expressed cautious support for the reformist junta that replaced the Salvadoran government, which was ousted in a military coup on October 15, 1979.

And in February 1980, as the persecution of the poor and the Church did not cease, he addressed an open letter to U.S. President Jimmy Carter in which he called upon the United States to discontinue military aid to the regime. "We are fed up with weapons and bullets," he pleaded.

Giving voice to the needs of the oppressed led to his assassination on March 24, 1980 while saying Mass. A death squad carrying out orders from the reactionary oligarchy that ruled over El Salvador shot archbishop Romero in the middle of the altar as soon as he finished his sermon.

In recognition of the role of Archbishop Romero in defense of human rights, the date of his assassination (24 March) was proclaimed in 2010 by the United Nations General Assembly as the 'International Day for the Right to the Truth Concerning Gross Human Rights Violations and for the Dignity of Victims.'

If liberation theology is a movement that embraces the poor and calls for social change by aiding the poor and oppressed through involvement in political and civic affairs, on the other hand, populism is, at its root, a belief in the power of regular people, and in their right to have control over their government rather than a small group of political insiders or a wealthy elite."

Speaking of the poor and social change, this is where liberation theology and populism are well connected.

Since the beginning of time, politicians from around the world have used the poor and the middle-class struggles for their political ends. Numerous times, they lure them with false promises to reach their ambitious goals.

What do the poor, the middle-class get when they elect these populist leaders?

From journalists, political commentators, businessmen to the ordinary people, they all agree that no election in the U.S. history, has ever attracted as much sexism, division, shame, commotion, and discussions as the 2016 presidential election.

Much of this tumult can be attributed to the Republican Presidential nominee, Donald Trump and his nasty remarks on women, racism and immigration."

In a rally in Michigan, a day after a new national poll shows that Hillary Clinton has taken a five-point lead over Donald Trump due to his poor performance at the First Presidential Debate on September 26, 2016, Trump ramped up his attacks on his opponent, the media, the politicians, and the lobbyists in Washington.

He quotes "The other day, one of the biggest people in that business, the very dishonest press business, they said Mr. Trump 'Did you really think you'd be here?' We're going to win the white house and it's going to be an awfully good November and that evening it's going to be a celebration. We're going to take on the special interests, the lobbyists and the powerful politicians that have stolen your jobs through theft and incompetence. They've stolen your wealth.

They're taking your middle class... On November 8, we are going to end Clinton's corruption. We had enough."

Without the middle-class and the poor, the wealthy top one percent would have not existed. The richest one percent use them as their pedestal to get richer.

However, the middle-class feels left out, cheated, abandoned and vulnerable. They are looking for a voice that understands their issues. Predators take advantage of their daily struggles.

A rich friend with whom I had an argument once, about the minimum wage being a pittance, told me "the poor could live with whatever they make. They don't know any better than the life they've been dealt with and have no dreams."

I was shocked by my friend's comment which represents sadly a broad view shared by lots of wealthy people who don't care about the poor and the middle class's financial challenges as long as their jobs are done.

Surely, you would understand why when fortune 500 companies go bankrupt, the CEO of these companies always pocket millions of dollars' bonuses while the middle-class workers are kicked out with nothing.

They just represent disposable workers or 'throwaway workers' like some labor economists used to call them.

Vicious politicians exploit their nagging conditions and the misery in which they wade with empty promises without a real plan to help them very much.

Is Donald Trump one of those billionaires who care about the financial difficulties facing the middle-class and the poor, or is he like the vicious politicians who take advantage of their struggles for their political ends?

Many people think the country is going to a wrong direction and they need some kind of change. However, the question is: "Is Donald Trump the right agent of change?"

The vice president, Joe Biden, referring to Donald Trump's income tax scandal published by the New York Times on October 1, 2016 quotes "Since when somebody who lives on top of the world in a penthouse overlooking the world, be in a position where he doesn't feel any obligation at all to pay any federal income tax, to support the military, to support education, to support our foreign policy? Since when is that patriotic? Can you imagine any other presidents who have said that and been proud of that?"

His comment illustrates lots of people's concerns about Donald Trump being the right agent of change, but also shows the extent of corruption in Washington where Congress passes mostly laws to benefit the wealthy.

Any ordinary people with an ordinary job who has done the same thing would be jailed for tax evasion.

This proves that the system is rigged and corrupt. A system built systematically to protect the interests of the wealthy like Donald Trump.

The question that each and every American should ask themselves: Is Donald Trump the right advocate for the poor and the middle class?

It's undeniable that he brings more people to the Republican Party, most of whom have never voted before.

If we consider the infatuation of hundreds and hundreds of voters who have registered on the night of the primaries and voted for Donald Trump in some precincts where, in the past elections, only a few republicans have voted, you would understand that the republican base see Donald Trump as "the messenger" due to his populist traditional views, which are bringing change to Washington, ending the status quo and business as usual.

When we have the republican base that considers Hillary Clinton as the epitome of the establishment and the status quo as she was painted by Bernie Sanders during the primaries before she became the first woman nominee of a major political party, it's imperative to understand why Donald Trump, with his message, embodies the trouble most republicans are living in.

Some of them think that Donald Trump can do a better job in working with the House and the Senate to achieve change for the American people who are yearning for change.

Referring to the populism concept which is a belief in the power of regular people, and in their right to have control over their government rather than a small group of political insiders or a wealthy elite, the question is: "Can Donald Trump - who is a part of the same wealthy and corrupt elite – really bring change to Washington?"

Speaking of populism, can Trump be characterized by this ideology?

The irony is, the United States Government has conducted a policy around the world that leads to the destruction of so many populist leaders when, in fact, they have one that has emerged right here under their nose, whom they are struggling to deal with.

Isn't this hypocrisy? Politicians who don't wash their dirty linen are peeking into their neighbors' dirty laundry.

UNITED STATES FOREIGN POLICY

Around the world, the United States have been accused of orchestrating many coup d'états that have almost overthrown or have ousted populist leaders whose interests differ from those of the U.S. Government.

In some cases, they work in the shadows to stop some populist leaders in some countries from getting elected due to conflict of interests.

Thus, the rise of Donald Trump makes people wonder why the establishment has failed to take action against the trumpist movement which has a striking similarity with all the populist movements that U.S. government has fought around the world.

Here are some examples.

During the Cold War, the U.S. has played a key role in destabilizing many democratically elected leaders or dictators from around the globe. United States involvement in regime change has continued beyond the Cold War and even after the Dissolution of the Soviet Union in many countries where they have installed friendly governments.

They have supported insurgencies and assassination attempts against some hostile regimes like Fidel Castro's failed attempt.

In many cases, they funnel millions of dollars into many countries to buy off anti-regime supporters and finance street protests. That was the case in Haiti. In 2004, the ousted president, Jean Bertrand Aristide, accused the United States and the Jamaican prime minister, P.J. Paterson of orchestrating a coup d'état against him.

It was rumored that the U.S. government was behind the military coup that overthrew the Muslim Brotherhood in Egypt.

With the help of the CIA, they have succeeded, in so many cases, to install their man as head of state.

The risk of leaving Iran open to the Soviet Union's aggression prompted the United States, under the supervision of the CIA, and the United Kingdom to plan and carry out the military coup that ousted in August 19, 1953 the Iranian Prime Minister, Mohammad Mosaddegh.

In fact, seeking to nationalize an Iranian oil industry operated by British companies, originated the coup that cost the prime minister his office along with his national front cabinet.

Any foreign political leader who seems to have a close tie to Russia represented a threat to the interests of the U.S. government. However, many still don't understand why the establishment hasn't done anything to stop Donald Trump who openly has a sympathy for Vladimir Putin who seeks to influence the 2016 U.S. election.

When Cuba became a communist country in the Western Hemisphere with the rise of Fidel Castro after he overthrew Fulgencio Batista in 1959, that was the biggest blow that the United States had ever received.

U.S. government had attempted to overthrow the communist regime that represented a threat to the region.

In 1965, when a young populist leader named José Francisco Peña Gómez went on radio and incited a popular uprising over the ouster of leftist Dominican leader Juan Bosch and demanded his return, U.S. President Lyndon Johnson ordered a military invasion with 23.000 Marines to prevent a Cuban-style revolution and protect the interests of the U.S. companies in the island.

They said the study of the past helps us comprehend the present.

Getting a closer look at the U.S. involvement in Chile when Salvador Allende, a socialist candidate, was elected President of this country in 1970 will make you understand what a slim chance it was for the senator of Vermont, Bernie Sanders, with his socialist views, to clinch the Democratic Party nomination.

From 1970 until the military coup on September 11, 1973 by General Augusto Pinochet against President Allende, the United States has not only plotted in vain prior coups with three different Chilean groups to which they had provided weapons but also strived to disrupt the Chilean economy.

It was not a secret that the policy adopted by Allende of nationalization of industries and collectivization originated the coup d'état which was sponsored by the United States Central Intelligence Agency (CIA).

History has showed us the involvement of the United States in so many countries around the globe where they conduct subversive activities to destroy populist leaders, among those the Haitian president Jean Bertrand Aristide and the Venezuelan president Hugo Chavez.

Both were anti-imperialist and criticized the US supported neoliberalism and laissez-faire capitalism. Both perceive that a democratic socialism is the only way to save the world and think, quote, "Democracy is impossible in a capitalist system because capitalism is the realm of injustice and a tyranny of the richest against the poorest".

Both spoke out against poverty, social injustice, assassinations and torture that seem to be the norm of a corrupt political system.

Roman Catholic priest, a proponent of liberation theology, Jean Bertrand Aristide became in 1991, Haiti's first democratically elected president. After 7 months in office, he was overthrown in a military coup by the Haitian army.

As for the Venezuelan president Hugo Chavez, after a failed coup d'état on April 11, 2002, he was restored after being ousted from office for 47 hours thanks to some military loyalists and support from the poor.

Considering the subversive actions led by the United States to destabilize many leaders whose political views and interests differ from those of the U.S government, the question that many anti-Trump are asking: how could the U.S. has not taken any actions to stop Donald Trump who openly praises the leader of Russia, Vladimir Putin and North Korean leader, Kim Jong-un?

In the meantime, a Trump supporter calls for a coup in case of a Hillary victory as it was published in the Boston Globe "'If she's in office, I hope we can start a coup. She should be in prison or shot." That is what Dan Bovman, a 50-year old contractor, said of Hillary Clinton, the Democratic nominee. "There's going to be a lot of bloodshed. But that's what it's going to take...I would do whatever I can for my country.'"

HOW TO STOP TRUMP

"I am sickened by what I heard today. Women are to be championed and revered, not objectified. I hope Mr. Trump treats this situation with the seriousness it deserves and works to demonstrate to the country that he has greater respect for women than this clip suggests."

Paul Ryan, Speaker of the House.

"No woman should ever be described in these terms or talked about in this manner. Ever."

Reince Priebus, Republican chairman.

"Hitting on married women? Condoning assaults? Such vile degradation demeans our wives and daughters and corrupt face to the world."

Tweets Mitt Romney

"Cindy and I will not vote for Donald Trump. I have never voted for a Democratic presidential candidate and we will not vote for Hillary Clinton. We will write in the name of some good conservative Republican who is qualified to be president," said the Arizona senator, John McCain, issuing a statement declaring that it's "impossible to continue to offer even conditional support for Trump."

"No way do I or would my father support this garbage. I am glad my father is not alive to watch this...He would tell us to vote the down ticket to stop Hillary. My father would not support this kind of campaign. If this is what the Republican Party wants, leave us Reagans out. Nancy would vote for HRC."

Michael Reagan.

Politics is not child's play. Whatever weapons you have at your disposal, you should sharpen it and use it to destroy your opponent in any way you can.

For instance, Donald Trump slammed Ted Cruz's father during the primaries when he said "His father was with Lee Harvey Oswald prior to Oswald being, you know, shot. I mean, the whole thing is ridiculous. What is this, right prior to his being shot and nobody even brings it up."

Not only Ted Cruz dropped out a few days after this comment even when he was encouraged by some political friends to stay in the race, but also he dropped a bombshell at the GOP convention by telling people to vote their conscience.

However, despite the RNC snub, he ended up endorsing Donald Trump months later; a move that many consider as a political suicide.

The winning instinct becomes such a powerful weapon that you must remove cast and stone to find any little dirt on your opponents and throw it at them.

Your opponents become an enemy that you must knock down.

Honesty does not prevail in politics. If survival is the rules of the jungle, winning, no matter what the cost, becomes the instinct of the politician.

Therefore, if you are a saint, politics is not for you.

What's happening in the American politics is unprecedented. Anyone can see that the electoral process and the institution of the American presidency is dragged to the mud, and has never been so low.

This election makes the world wonder if true democracy really exists. People from around the globe use to think that politics was done differently in the United States and that politicians here put the interests of the country above their personal ambitions.

That is not true.

Insulting one another, a nasty campaign filled with scandals are what characterize the 2016 election. It has become a TV reality show.

The American people are witnessing a street battle they have never seen before and hope they will never see something like this again in a lifetime.

The choice between those two candidates is not clear yet. They try to choose the lesser of the two evils. The American people are lost between the historical first female democratic nominee, Hillary Clinton, and the outsider real estate mogul billionaire, Donald Trump.

Most democrat or republican voters are driven by the fear that the other candidate might win.

Real issues that matter to the American people such as jobs creation, the economy, how to defeat ISIS, the minimum wages, health care, criminal justice reforms are lost in a battle for the conquest of the White House.

The libertarian candidate, Gary Johnson, and the green party candidate, Jill Stein, seem to not offer an alternative as they struggle to reach 10 percent in the polls. The first one, unfortunately, had a brain freeze since he could not remember the name of a foreign leader that he likes or the meaning of Aleppo; and the second one does not support vaccine due perhaps to her religious beliefs.

The people are torn between the two most unpopular candidates in the American history.

One is accused of corruption and smearing some of her husband's accusers; and the other one is facing accusations of racism, misogyny, sexual assault, and groping women without their consent.

The release by WikiLeaks of thousands of John Podesta's emails - including excerpts of Hillary Clinton's paid remarks to Wall Street in which she mentioned that she needs "both a public and a private position" – makes you understand why 60 percent of American think Hillary Clinton is untrustworthy to become president.

Stating on the campaign trail that she would never "let wall street wreck main street again and no CEO is too big to jail", many think her public position concerning main street is just a speech to put baby to sleep since her private position is that the financial reform "really has to come from the industry itself."

The question is: Can any financial reform come from Wall Street whose greedy CEO caused the crash of 2008?

In the American political history, no one has ever seen the nominee of a political party waging war on the leaders of his own party because they feel they could no longer support him due to his inappropriate behavior.

That's the case of the Republican nominee, Donald Trump who tweets on October 11, 2016: "It is so nice that the shackles have been taken off me and I can now fight for America the way I want to."

This tweet is followed by another one stating "Democrats – with the exception of cheating Bernie out of the nom- have always proven to be far more loyal to each other than the Republicans."

Trump's last tweet shows clearly the animosity between the nominee and the leaders of his own party.

"Disloyal R's are far more difficult than Crooked Hillary. They come at you from all sides. They don't know how to win – I will teach them!"

After the publication by the Washington Post of a 2005 video clip in which you can hear Trump brag about groping women without their consent, how he "grabs them by their pussy" to use his own words, and they allow him to do it because "when you're a star, you can do anything.'

This has caused a growing number of elected Republicans to withdraw their support to their party nominee, Donald Trump, and demand him to step down.

However, he vows that he will never drop out and let his supporters down.

RNC is stuck and so is Mike Pence.

Meanwhile, after the second presidential debate and following the access Hollywood leaked tape, eleven women have come forward and accused Trump of sexual assault.

The candidate threatens to sue his accusers after the election.

He slams these mounting allegations against him and calls it "lies and smears" while insinuating that the media and Clinton camp are behind attacks.

Although 67% of American believe that Trump made unwanted advances to those women, Trump supporters are sticking to their leader and said they will still vote for him.

Struggling in the polls in some battleground states and nationally, his wife, Melania Trump, broke her silence two days before the last presidential debate to defend her husband's comment as 'locker room talk' and accused the Clinton Camp and the media of working against her husband.

Is that move can make him gain back the independent women that he has never targeted?

The way Mrs. Trump referred to Billy Bush strangely reminds me of some parents, when their kid did something wrong, they automatically put the blame on the other kids they usually hang out with.

However, Billy Bush was suspended and later lost his job at NBC due to the leaked tape.

Although Trump has never been doing well among women who don't trust him according to many polls, the leaked tape has affected his chance even more among white college educated women, largely in the suburbs, who have always voted Republican in the presidential elections for the past sixty years.

HOW TO PREVENT A TRUMP PRESIDENCY

In the American history, we have never seen a presidential candidate so decried like Donald Trump. Most party leaders are disgusted by his nomination that they see, among others, as a threat to U.S. national security. Many think that it is time to think about the country over the party.

Astonishing is the defection among the party leaders who openly endorse the democratic nominee, Hillary Clinton, claiming their party nominee, Trump, is unfit to be president.

Isn't this an unprecedented event?

Since the beginning, many Republican leaders like Mitt Romney have been waging a red flag warning people about the political dangers posed by Trump, but people did not want to listen.

Those like New Jersey Governor Chris Christie, the party chairman Reince Priebus, the House Speaker Paul Ryan and others who are hopped aboard the Trump train continue to defend his racially and nationalistic rhetoric despite his attacks on women, the disabled, the prisoner of war, John McCain, the Muslims, the Latino immigrants, the Syrian refugees, the Gold Star parents.

However, sixteen GOP leaders cut ties with Trump after lewd comments. President Obama campaigning for Hillary said, quote "You can't have it both ways," hammering the GOP leaders like Paul Ryan who stated that he will not campaign for Trump but still endorses the party nominee.

The fissures in the Republican party are so deep that many experts already predict that it will be difficult for the party to reunify after the presidential elections.

Donald Trump has created a base of supporters so strong that they swallow everything he said.

Railing against powerful corporations, political dynasties, the dishonest media and a political corrupt system, he has succeeded to create a political movement and make his supporters, mainly the white working class and blue collar workers, believe that the election is rigged and they will rig it at the polling booths.

His surrogates like Newt Gingrich, former mayor Rudolph Giuliani echoed his claims. President Obama scorned Trump to "Stop whining." Many GOP leaders condemned his allegations. Paul Ryan brushed it off with a strong statement "Our democracy relies on confidence in election results, and the speaker is fully confident the states will carry out this election with integrity."

Machiavellian populist, he has succeeded to ignite a civil war inside the GOP. Many of his supporters view Republican Paul Ryan and many others who distance themselves from Trump as traitors.

Can Ryan keep his job as speaker of the house after November 8 when some GOP leaders do not agree with his position of not campaigning with Trump?

The Maine Governor Paul LePage, a Trump supporter, stated, quote "We need Donald Trump to show some authoritarian power in our country and bring back the rule of law."

Doesn't authoritarian power equal dictatorship?

Following his proposed plan of banning Muslims from entering the country in the wake of the deadly terror attack in San Bernardino, California, the British Prime Minister, David Cameron, said, quote "I think his remarks are divisive, stupid and wrong and I think if he came to visit our country I think it'd unite us all against him."

Despite the widespread doubts and emails scandals confronting Hillary Clinton which could make the democratic nominee an easy take for any other republican presidential candidate, Trump has been struggling, since he clinched the nomination last May, to expand his coalition beyond 40 percent according to different surveys.

Although Trump suggests that Hillary is dishonest and crooked and got a pass with her emails scandals because of the Obama administration and the collusion that exists between the State Department and the department of Justice (DOJ), he is still trailing Hillary Clinton in the polls.

Fearing to retain their congressional majority in case of an imminent defeat of Trump, the release of the lewd Trump's audio tape not only plunges the

Republican Party into chaos a month before the election but could undermine the entire Republican ticket in November.

Given that their majority in the House 246-to-186 might be in jeopardy, and worried that Trump's controversial position on trade, immigration and other issues might hurt down-ballot GOP candidates in November, the Speaker of the House, Paul Ryan, released this statement "Paul Ryan is focusing the next month on defeating Democrats, and all Republicans running for office should probably do the same."

In fact, this was the concern, back in August 11, 2016, of 111 former Republican who have sent a draft letter to the RNC that read 'Only the immediate shift of all available RNC resources to vulnerable Senate and House races will prevent the GOP from drowning with a Trump-emblazoned anchor around its neck.'

The position of some Republican leaders who distance themselves to their party nominee upsets a cornered, vengeful and selfish Trump who promises to teach them a lesson.

Trump's reaction reminds me of a Haitian outsider, back in 2010, who ran a nasty campaign in Haiti.

What some Republican leaders had failed to do was to unseat Trump at the convention party as it was suggested by the never Trump movement group which had drafted their own presidential candidate.

And now those same leaders – like Speaker Paul D. Ryan and Senate Majority Leader Mitch McConnell - are paying the price for lining up behind the devil who viciously attacks them as losers, weak and ineffective because they came to a breaking point where they should choose between the interest of the party or Trump.

Trump claimed at a rally in Florida that there was a "sinister deal" behind the republican revolt and that he "will figure it out."

Some see Trump unfounded accusations as a desperate move to warn the Republican leaders of the consequences of their actions if they continue to abandon his wagon at a crucial moment when he needs their support like he said based on his performance at the second debate.

Others already foreseen no winning chance for the party nominee shift their focus on keeping the majority of the House and the Senate.

Newt Gingrich, former Speaker of the House and Trump's surrogate, sounded off the Republican leaders who abandoned Trump's sinking boat saying, quote "The only question we should ask every Republican is not you're going to support Donald Trump. Are you going to help beat Hillary Clinton? Any Republican who is willing to help her should join the Democratic Party."

This election has unveiled to the world the dirty side of the American democracy. The same dirty tricks politicians abroad master were efficiently used by the Democratic establishment to get rid of Bernie Sanders and make sure he did not win the primaries.

If Bernie Sanders has created a vast socialist movement that could have shaped the political system if he has reached his goal, on the other hand, Donald Trump's populist movement scares many who see him as a threat, a catastrophe that, no matter what, we should stop.

WHY ARE PEOPLE DRIVEN BY TRUMP RHETORIC?

"Of all the storms that roiled America in the Obama era, few, if any, have been more consistently underestimated or more persistent than the Great Populist Putsch...The tidal wave of grassroots rage that rose out of the wreckage of the 2008 crash and Bush presidency has variously spawned the tea party, Occupy Wall Street, the Bernie Sanders revolution, and the Donald Trump insurgency. Yet for much of the way, the elites of both political parties were often slow to grasp what was happening, and Barack Obama was no exception."

Frank Rich

"We have a large public that is very ignorant about public affairs and very susceptible to simplistic slogans by candidates who appear out of nowhere, have no track record, but mouth appealing slogans."

Zbigniew Brzeziński

"I think many of the issues in the American campaign mirror those happening in the rest of politics, certainly in the United Kingdom and rest of Europe right now, elements to do with the rise of populism, strong movements, insurgent movements are left and right, the center feeling under attack and on the defensive, are many of the same issues, actually."

"...The Donald Trump phenomenon in the U.S. is mirrored completely by the Brexit phenomenon in the U.K. It's very similar forces. And what is interesting to me is there are two different groups that come together, who don't really agree with each other, but have come together in unity against, if you like, what is perceived as the status quo, or - and certainly what is a more center-right or center-left type of politics.

Tony Blair, former UK PM

The rise of Trump in the presidential race come as a shock to many people in the United States and around the world. Rebellious and high temper, controversial figure whose racist remarks draw international condemnation, he took over the Republican Party and has created a movement that will drive the party into the abyss.

Voicing the anger of a Republican base that nourishes an irrational hatred of anything associated

with President Obama and has a distrust in the party establishment who, they think, neglect them and sell them out at every term, Trump comes along as the shepherd of a flock of stray sheep.

His xenophobic and bigoted rhetoric and his unrealistic proposed policies found common ground amongst the white blue collar and the white working-class who are dissatisfied with Washington.

If his protectionism and isolationism foreign policy proposals draw worries among U.S. allies, on the other hand, it resonates with white working-class voters that have felt marginalized for years by a party which they perceive as the party of the wealthy due to its policies among those, cut taxes for the top 1 percent as a way to create jobs and unleash economic growth.

Is this a joke? Many wonder as Trump makes racial comments, building a wall, and a mass deportation of millions of immigrants the signature of his campaign.

If people believe that Bernie Sanders' movement was going to give rise to a revolution that would have changed America socially and economically, Trump's movement resembles so far a movement initiated by the Haitian president Jean Bertrand Aristide whose supporters were as angry as those of Trump.

Tired of political correctness, and beat down by a system that does not care about them, they have longed for a savior, someone they can identify with. And Donald Trump becomes their voice as they embark as trumpists in a vast movement that apparently will give them back everything they are entitled to.

Saying out loud what they used to say behind closed doors, Trump becomes one of the most political figure that America has never produced.

If his rallies, during the primaries, drew thousands of Trumpists who are inspired by their leader's slogan "Make America Great Again," some of his events have also been the scene of violent incidents where his supporters and anti-protesters clashed on the streets in the worst chaotic scenes people have never witnessed in the American history.

If Trump always put the blame on Bernie Sanders' supporters claiming they were paid and sent to disrupt his events, he was also criticized for encouraging and praising violence against protesters at his public rallies: "...So if you see somebody getting ready to throw tomatoes, knock the crap out of him, would you, seriously? I will pay for the legal fees, I promise."

The Republican Party is divided between the Trumpists and the anti-Trump. 50 GOP National security advisers sent a letter to stop Trump and warn that he will be a reckless president.

Trump, as usual, quickly dismissed the snub. "These are 50 people who have been running our country forever. They said we can't support Donald Trump. The reason they can't. You know why? I'm not gonna hire these people. I don't want these people."

As a growing number of Republicans are dismayed over Trump's continuous reckless comments, and view his emergence as a populist demagogue who fills his supporters with empty promises, he struggles to keep his party in line and does not strike conciliatory tone with the party leaders.

His erratic behavior comforts some worldwide leaders who come to realize that they're not the only ones with an insane political system and crazy politicians. Many observers predict that a Trump's presidency would alienate some American allies and weaken the nation.

THE SAME CAUSES PRODUCE THE SAME EFFECTS IN THE SAME CIRCUMSTANCES

Under president Georges W. Bush, United States has faced one of the greatest economic depression that was best known as the late-2000s financial crisis originated by the war in Iraq that has engendered regional instability and a weakened world economy.

Though the public favored the 2003 Iraq war which was initially intended to be a quick in-and-out operation, but the lack of weapons of mass destruction, the length and the post-war occupation became a turning point in the American public opinion who were politically divided over the real causes of the war.

The impact it had on the U.S. economy was so devastated that many Americans wondered if it was worth the loss of American lives and the billions of dollars spent.

As the long-term military presence in Iraq has cost the U.S. more than a trillion dollars in debt, 2007 marked the worst housing market crash that engendered a multidimensional financial crisis in U.S. history.

Thousands of Americans lost their jobs due the collapse of the economy that drove many employers to file bankruptcy. Increased foreclosure rates among homeowners reached an alarming point as Wall Street investors increased the risk of a nationwide recession.

Amidst the post Iraqi war turmoil, in 2006, the Democrats had regained control of the House and the Senate. And the Democratic Controlled Congress has begun to restrict spending on the war while enacting a new agenda that included health care reform, stimulus spending and Wall Street reform.

More than half of Americans turned on President Bush whose approval rating in 2007 fell below 40 percent, according to news polls. Unemployment rate skyrocketed. People were struggling to make ends meet.

During this political and economic disarray, came along senator Barack Obama, a fierce opponent of the Iraq War. His populist slogan of change and hope resonated with every single American.

His charisma has won over White, Hispanic and Black. Enthused, thousands of college students as of the rest of the nation hopped on board the Obama train. He surprised the world to become the first black President in November 4, 2008 of a nation whose history of racial segregation was still engraved in the people mind.

He inherited an unprecedented financial crisis that many economists compared to the great depression. Many major corporations filed bankruptcy, one by one. Thousands of workers were laid off. The U.S. auto industries and some major banks were collapsing. The country was hit hard economically and the U.S. stock market has reached its lowest point which plunged the world into worries.

Something needed to be done quickly to 'stem the economic downturn,' according to many economists.

On February 2009, to revive the economy, a stimulus package of $787 billion was negotiated and approved despite some opposition in both chambers.

The bill which provided $212 billion - or 27% - for tax breaks for individuals and businesses was intended to quote President Obama "...create jobs, but jobs doing the work America needs to be done: repairing our infrastructure, modernizing our schools and hospitals, and promoting the clean, alternative energy sources that will help us finally declare independence from foreign oil."

The stimulus package may have benefited some people but others considered it was more beneficial to the big corporations.

Many observers believe the historical compromises that the House, Senate and White House struck to finalize the American Recovery and Reinvestment Act of 2009 triggered the tea party movement that not only opposed government-sponsored universal healthcare (Obamacare) but also called for a reduction of the U.S. national debt and federal budget deficit by reducing government spending and for lower taxes.

Isn't the U.S. national debt a result of borrowing to pay for the cost of the Iraq war?

The Tea Party movement has organized many protests, including the taxpayer march on Washington on September 12, 2009.

Dissatisfaction with mainstream Republican Party leaders initiated this grassroots movement that has triggered a civil war within the GOP.

If the tea party movement was a rebellious uprising that has shaken the structural foundation of the party, the establishment, occupied to satisfy the desires of the donors instead of the voters, never took time to seek the cause that has produced the uprising and make some real changes.

Meantime, as President Obama finished his first term, some people concluded that he did not materialize his campaign promises and did not see no improvement in their conditions of life.

Losing the support of a large majority, including some college students that have largely contributed to his first election, President Obama, in 2012, targeted the gay communities and the Latinos which helped him tremendously get reelected.

In response of the support of those groups, President Obama fought hard to have the gay marriage legalized. However, his comprehensive immigration reform was blocked by Republicans in the House of Representatives; and later the Supreme Court was deadlocked on that bipartisan legislation.

Time is a key factor in politics. If national polls showed in 2010 that public opinion favored an immigration reform, that general view has shifted in 2016.

Capitalizing on the fear that a vast majority of the lower middle-class has toward immigrants who, they think, are taking their jobs, Trump becomes the sailor of a sinking boat.

Trump's rise not only opposes everything that America stands for: moral values, but also surprises everyone who always thought that no outsider could ever flourish in the American political landscape.

Trump's phenomenon is not something new. When people are angry, fed up with the status quo, dissatisfied with the corrupt traditional politicians, and the ruling class which they perceive as a gang whose goal is to get richer at their expense, they always turn to an outsider whose message is appealing.

Besides anti-trade, anti-immigrant policy and bringing jobs back to America that draw the blue-collar workers and the white working class toward Trump, fear of the nonwhite population that will become in a near future a majority is the main factor that prompts Trump to prominence.

Bernie Sanders along with Trump movement have shown the political polarization and the vulnerability of American society to new ideologies.

As the Vatican had failed to understand the disconnect between the church hierarchy and the members which led to a growing number of church members to embrace a new religion, the failure of Washington along with the GOP establishment has created the trumpism, a movement that could turn everything upside down.

Many think that the GOP should be worried about this movement.

Unfortunately, some GOP congress members flip flop on Trump only for political purposes. Evan McMullin, Utah's third-party candidate stated "Donald Trump has pulled the party away from conservative values. He has pulled the party towards populism and towards white nationalism."

Will Trump's movement give rise to a plethora of political parties in a near future?

Only time will tell.

TRUMP VERSUS THE MEDIA

"The election is being rigged by corrupt media, pushing completely false allegations and outright lies in an effort to elect her president. But we are going to stop it. But we're not going to back down."

Donald Trump.

"Today we live in a society in which spurious realities are manufactured by the media, by governments, by big corporations, by religious groups...So I ask, in my writing, What is real? Because unceasingly we are bombarded with pseudo-realities manufactured by very sophisticated people using very sophisticated electronic mechanisms. I do not distrust their motives; I distrust their power. They have a lot of it. And it is an astonishing power: that of creating whole universes, universes of the mind. I ought to know. I do the same thing.

Philip K. Dick

"The media's the most powerful entity on earth. They have the power to make the innocent guilty and to make the guilty innocent, and that's power. Because they control the minds of the masses."

Malcolm X

"The media is a mirror of the society. The media is not merchandise that can be imported. The media originates from the nations and it's the mirror of the culture of the represented society. An intelligent, intellectual and open-minded society with a rich culture is reflected in its media. Meanwhile the media of a society full of ignorance, prejudices, hatred and conspiracies represents these features in itself."

George Kurdahi

Since the beginning of time, the media has always been the target of left-wing, right-wing or centrist politicians.

In many countries around the world, freedom of speech has led to persecution, imprisonment, and even assassination of journalists.

Intimidation becomes a useful weapon to shut off many journalists from speaking out as some newspapers, TV or radio stations are ransacked, burnt down or have their windows smashed.

Totalitarian governments always seek total control of the media in order to control people's minds.

Journalists are often accused of being paid to tarnish opposition leaders or the government in office.

The social media has influenced so much the way people get their news that nowadays the media is fighting to survive. They must dig to find some shocking news that can attract the readers or the viewers.

It is sad to say that some sordid stories sometimes put journalists in the line of fire. Politicians often accused them of not being neutral and fair, and being negative.

This is the case of Trump's pro-sexual comments caught on tape. Did the media give too much coverage to those women who came forward and accused him of sexual misconduct or less coverage to the Clinton emails scandals?

Did the media coverage reflect a neutral position in both cases?

The liberal media is being hammered by Trump and his surrogates for too much coverage of this case that has damaged Trump campaign at some point. Even Newt Gingrich went into a heated exchange with Fox News anchor Megyn Kelly for covering the leaked access Hollywood tape, saying "You are fascinated with sex."

Isn't Megyn Kelly working for a news organization that's promoting the trumpist movement?

Politicians always want to have control over what information they want the public to be exposed to.

The role of the media is to report the news accurately and impartially to keep us informed. However, it's often been criticized of partisanship because of the excessive coverage of some stories that might be destructive for a candidate or a government running a country.

The same information can be distorted depending on which media outlets it comes from in order to influence the public as they take side. Some news organizations turn clearly and openly into a propaganda machine for some political party.

How does the media coverage shape or influence people's opinion? Can a journalist be neutral when he works for a news organization that caters to liberal or conservative lines?

The media has an immense power, but its power is often besmirched by politicians who accuse them of being to quote Trump "dishonest and corrupt."

If you speak to a Trump supporter, he will tell you that he's never seen a more abusively bias one sided pro Hillary media in his entire life while Hillary supporters think they should stop attacking the free press for doing their jobs.

The question most people are asking: Are the news media clearly bias as they are being accused of?

DENIGRATE THE MEDIA, FOR WHAT PURPOSES?

The 2016 U.S. election takes place in a very particular context. The global terrorist threat and the strengthening of radical Islam have worried the world more than ever as France, Turkey, Belgium have been the scenes of deadly terrorist attacks that killed hundreds of people. Even the United States has been under attack by homegrown terrorists.

Although the Syrian crisis, tensions in the South China Sea, North Korea persistent nuclear missile test, ISIS and the offensive of the Iraqi army led by U.S. coalition forces to retake Mosul become breaking news, however, they have not attracted so much media coverage than the 2016 U.S. election.

Most of this can be attributed to the drama surrounding both candidates.

Trump has attracted so much media coverage due to his incoherent and controversial statements that it was difficult for other candidates to put their word out during the primaries.

Unconventional candidate who is running a nasty campaign against Washington and the political establishment, Trump never stops slamming the media whether on twitter or at his political rallies where journalists are often harassed by his supporters.

Trump hammers the media at every occasion and even brags about it in his tweet "CNN just doesn't get it, and that's why their ratings are so low – and getting worse. Boring anti-trump panelists, mostly losers in life."

Or in that tweet against the media for reporting the story of a woman who claimed being kissed by

Trump at one of his hotels "The media has gone too far in making this false accusation. There is no way something like this would have happened in a public place on Mother's Day at Mr. Trump's resort. The reality is this: For the media to wheel out a politically motivated democratic activist with a legal dispute against the same resort owned by Mr. Trump."

Sadly, the media has always been blamed for any politician misstep as if they are the ones that are fabricating the stories they're reporting.

"100 % fabricated and made-up charges, pushed strongly by the media and the Clinton Campaign, may poison the minds of the American Voter. FIX!" tweets Trump who ties the liberal medias to the Clinton Camp.

If you asked most Americans what is their view about the media, you would be surprised to see that Americans trust in the media has hit an historic low.

Most people don't believe what they are hearing on the evening news and they think most of what they are hearing on TV is bias. Therefore, they turn to social media to get their news.

Trump's constant attacks on the news organizations impact the news media lowest ratings. A survey shows that only 32% of Americans believe that the news media "report the news fully, accurately and fairly" while only 14% of Republicans think the media is fair.

At a certain point, he has succeeded to destroy the credibility of any credible media outlet.

The question we should ask: Doesn't Trump always have his events covered when he hurls insults at all kinds of people?

Trump never spares a single time to launch attacks on the press and reporters by calling them names ranging from "sleazy, dishonest to the worst human beings he has ever met."

On the eve of a fundraising event he had organized for veterans' groups in which he collected $5.6 million, he held a news conference to talk about the event but spent the entire time insulting reporters instead.

The CPJ board (Committee to Protect Journalists) is alarmed by Trump behavior which deliberately creates a hostile environment for reporters covering his rallies. The CPJ chairman declares a Trump presidency would create an "unprecedented threat to the rights of journalists and to CPJ's ability to advocate for press freedom around the world."

If they are journalists in the mainstream media that can't stand Donald Trump and viscerally believe that he represents a threat to the United States if he ever becomes elected, they are entitled to their opinion.

My former journalism professor once told me that "Freedom of speech is just a myth and each individual is entitled to his own political view although a journalist is supposed to be neutral."

Thus, neutrality is just unrealistic.

Intimidation and persecution of journalists always tend to destroy the regimes that practice them.

Therefore, politicians have developed a new weapon that is more powerful and efficient than any weapon in the world.

It is called 'calumny' to discredit the press and the reporters.

Trump has reached his goal by mastering this weapon.

THE POLLS

"The American people, Neil, are sick and tired of excuses. They are sick and tired of the blame game. And they're sick and tired of the deception coming from this president and this administration. This is why I believe that I am doing so well in the polls."

Herman Cain

"There is a garbage culture out there, where we pour garbage on people. Then the pollsters run around and take a poll and say, do you smell anything?"

Bob Woodward

"Polling is merely an instrument for gauging public opinion. When a president or any other leader pays attention to poll results, he is, in effect, paying attention to the views of the people. Any other interpretation is nonsense."

George Gallup

"The election is absolutely being rigged by the dishonest and distorted media pushing Crooked Hillary – but also at many polling places – SAD"

Donald Trump

An undecided voter I spoke with describes this election as a basket containing sweet and rotten apples. The irony is, the voters unfortunately picked the two rotten apples over the sweet ones.

Studies have demonstrated that 60% of voters' decisions are relatively affected by candidate qualities, however Hillary Clinton and Donald Trump are the most unlikeable and unfavorable candidates United States has ever had.

No candidate has ever been so obsessed and concerned about the polls than Donald Trump in the political circles. When he lags far behind Hillary, he claims that the polls are rigged and the pollsters are screwing them in favor of Hillary Clinton so she can win.

When the polls show him struggling in key battleground states, he slams the media and tells his supporters not to believe in them.

Some of his surrogates latch onto the idea that the pollsters are trying to deflate those supporters who think Trump can win.

Remember the statement that he made during the primaries when he was dominating the polls "I love the poorly educated. ...We're gonna win so much we'll be sick of winning."

In recent history, the polling industry has never faced such critical challenges and spurred so much discussion and debate across the electorate. While many people question the accuracy of the polls, some others wonder if the polls are not fabricated.

"Brexit" pre-election polls, for example, did raise questions in people's minds about the reliability and the scientific basis of certain polls' conclusions.

It is unsurprising that lots of Trumpists don't believe in the polls. Billy Graham statement about the church illustrates the Trumpists' view about the polling industry. Graham quotes "Many churches of all persuasions are hiring research agencies to poll neighborhoods, asking what kind of church they prefer. Then the local churches design themselves to fit the desires of the people. True faith in God that demands selflessness is being replaced by trendy religion that serves the selfish."

If you are a Trumpist, you have probably wondered why even bother to vote since the polls negative projections have already showed the unviability about a Trump Presidency.

Thus, do you understand why Trump and his surrogates are waging a war against the media and the pollsters as if they are faking the polls?

Although most voters have already made up their minds, can the drama surrounding both candidates influence the polls?

You surely remember how tight was the race between Hillary and Trump before the access Hollywood leaked tape.

Its effect has been devastating for Trump whose polls number have dropped considerably and showed him trailing Hillary by 8 or 5 points.

As all hope was lost for Trump, and Hillary camp already celebrating her imminent victory, the F.B.I. director James B. Comey gave Trump a golden gift with an announcement that the agency is reopening Clinton probe after new emails was found in Anthony Weiner sexting case.

Top members of Congress were informed by Comey in a letter that the bureau had "learned of the existence of emails that appear to be pertinent to the investigation."

Doesn't the old saying "Nothing happens for nothing" illustrate Comey's actions at eight days of the general election?

Trump, capitalizing on the latest news, has regained momentum. "Clinton' s corruption is on scale we have never seen before," Trump said.

Neither Podesta's Russian hacked emails nor his pay for play allegations about the Clinton Foundation and the State Department while Hillary was in office have never rescued Trump campaign like Comey's bombshell.

Nevertheless, the ABC/WaPo poll shows him with a slim one-point lead; and in a new national tracking poll taken at seven days of the general election Hillary Clinton and Donald Trump are neck-and-neck.

Once again, Donald Trump and his surrogates love the polls.

And now it's the democrats turn to claim that the media is lying about the polls to push the voters to go and vote.

CAN TRUMP WIN?

The race is very tightening in some key states, according to the latest polls. Either candidate needs 270 electoral votes to win.

No candidate has ever won the presidential elections without the support of African-American and Latino voters.

Although almost 24 million people have already cast their ballot in early vote, the African-American vote in some key states is down. Hillary is trying to secure the undecided voters by releasing new ads to target the Latinos and African-Americans.

The lack of enthusiasm among African-Americans and millennials for Hillary Clinton drives President Obama, his wife, and other surrogates like Bernie Sanders to embark on the campaign trail to appeal to the black voters and the undecided so they can get them out and vote to prevent the country from going backward.

A plethora of superstars like Pharrell, Jay Z, Stevie Wonder, are also on the campaign trail with Hillary Clinton.

On the other hand, Donald Trump is trying a different strategy by encouraging democrats who already cast their ballots to switch their votes since it is legal to do so in seven states which include Wisconsin, Minnesota, Michigan, Pennsylvania, New York, Connecticut, Mississippi.

Within five days of general election, he's been disciplined and stayed on message "Nice and cool Trump, he repeated" as he read from a teleprompter. Painting Hillary Clinton as a criminal who will be eventually indicted if elected is a strategy that he's using to discourage her supporters from going to the polling booths on November 8.

Is this going to work when the trumpism is painted as a movement against welfare, people of color and immigrants.?

Although the Trumpists are enthusiastic compared to Hillary Supporters, are they enough to get Trump elected?

Only 3% of African-Americans support Donald Trump. The lack of support among that group for Trump is understandable.

Recently we have witnessed many cases where police brutality, racial profiling, misconduct and shootings of unarmed African-Americans had sparked rage and wild demonstrations around the country.

Those shootings draw condemnation from many officials who deeply think a police reform is imperative in this country. However, Donald Trump not only laid out his plan about the stop and frisk which he thinks is necessary to keep the inner cities safe, but presents himself as the "Law and Order" candidate.

His message "What do you have to lose? "doesn't resonate to the African-American communities.

The lack of respect for women does not resonate well with college students that have been raped or exposed to rape victims on campuses. His reckless mouth and his actions toward women reflect the lack of support among white women with a college degree.

Can his wife's message appeal to that group at five days of the election?

Since the beginning of his candidacy in June 2015, Trump has made his opposition to the Latinos a centerpiece of his campaign. He had insulted and vilified the immigrants from Mexico that he labeled "rapists and criminals." "When Mexico sends his people, they're

not sending their best. They're not sending you. They're sending people that have lots of problems, and they're bringing those problems with us. They're bringing drugs. They're bringing crime. They're rapists. And some, I assume, are good people."

All along his campaign, he's been pivoting on immigration issues in an attempt to placate the millions of Latinos he had already offended. His trip to Mexico to meet with the Mexican president has not succeeded to soften his image.

His insulting remarks towards Mexicans explain the lack of support he has among Hispanic voters. That also explains why an increase number of Latinos have become American citizens to prevent a Trump's presidency.

At this point, lots of Republicans anxious about a Trump's victory share the view of Trump super Pac chair, Ed Rollins who stated "If somehow Trump pulls a miracle comeback here, which would take a miracle at this point, then obviously it's his party, he can do what he wants with it. If not, I think we begin from ground zero and with lots of different factions and lots of different candidates."

DÉJÀ VU

"I have never seen in my lifetime or in modern political history any presidential candidate trying to discredit the elections and the election process before votes have even taken place. It's unprecedented. It happens to be based on no facts..."

President Obama

"Leaders are responsible not for running public opinion polls but for the consequences of their actions."

Henry A. Kissinger

"As long as God continues to breathe into my body, nothing can surprise me in this world."

Mario Chateau

History does nothing but repeat itself. It is often remarked that the same sort of events that had occurred before somewhere in the world can recur at any time in another part of the globe.

Donald J. Trump's emergence bears a striking similarity with the rise of a Haitian president, Joseph Michel Martelly.

On October 16, 2016, a North Carolina GOP headquarter was burned down overnight by someone who threw a bottle containing a flammable liquid through a window while an anti-GOP slogan referring to "Nazi Republican" was spray-painted on a nearby wall.

And on the evening of November 1, 2016, a Black Missionary Baptist church was torched in Mississippi with "Vote Trump" painted on the wall.

A pro-Trump white nationalist made a robocall in Utah against a third-party candidate, Evan McMullin. He quotes "Hello. My name is William Johnson. I am a farmer and a white nationalist. I make this call against Evan McMullin and in support of Donald Trump. Evan McMullin is an open borders, amnesty supporter. Evan has two mommies. His mother is a lesbian – married to another woman. Evan is okay with that. Indeed, Evan supports the Supreme Court ruling legalizing gay marriage. Evan is over 40-years-old and is not married and doesn't even have a girlfriend. I believe Evan is a closet homosexual. Don't vote for Evan McMullin. Vote for Donald Trump."

In a few states, such as North Carolina, Republicans trying to suppress minority votes so they could win, raise concern for democrats.

Those are breaking news that shock the American electorate, however, these things are the norms in many countries during elections season.

In modern political history, Trump has not been the only one who tries to discredit the elections and the election process before votes have even taken place. His conspiratorial and fact-free rhetoric that the elections could be rigged against him at the voting booths are voiced by his surrogates.

Top Donald Trump adviser, Rudy Giuliani, backing up the candidate's comments on rigged election said "Dead people generally vote for Democrats rather than Republicans...You want me to say that I think the election in Philadelphia and Chicago is going to be fair? I would have to be a moron to say that."

Those allegations are nothing than a strategy to contest the election results, and inspire post-election violence.

These tactics were used in Haiti by Michel Joseph Martelly, an outsider, an entertainer, a businessman who ran for president.

People from all over the world thought that was a joke knowing the man reckless mouth and his past.

He launched a nasty campaign against the traditional politicians, the ruling class and the media. He promised to end government corruption, to "drain the swamp" like Trump said.

In the November 2010 election, preliminary results that were published by CEP in early December gave the lead to Mirlande Manigat with 31 percent of the vote that set her up for a runoff election against Jude Celestin who came second with 22 percent.

Several candidates, including Michel Martelly who finished in third place, accused the Préval administration and CEP (Provisional Electoral Council) of committing massive fraud and called for the election annulment.

The U.S. Embassy criticized the preliminary results saying Haitian, U.S. and other international monitors had predicted that Celestin was likely to be eliminated in the first round.

Martelly better known as Sweet Micky called his supporters to demonstrate. The country was paralyzed for three straight days and several properties were destroyed by his supporters who set barricades and political offices ablaze.

Gunfire erupted in some cities across the country.

The Organization of American States (OEA) and other international monitors intervened in vain to resolve the crisis.

Amidst this social upheaval, Secretary of State, Hillary Clinton, threatened President Préval that Congress would cut off aid to Haiti if he did not force his close ally, Jude Celestin, to drop out.

Martelly was soon given the second place in the runoff. And In march 2011, he won the election against all odds.

The singer president mocked the press and even released a song in which he insulted some journalists individually.

The similarity between the 2010 Haitian election and the 2016 U.S. election is very striking.

Both Mirlande Manigat and Hillary Clinton are attorneys and former First Ladies. However, Trump and Martelly not only share the same reckless mouth, but also came as outsiders from the political circles.

In addition to their volatile character, both are entertainers and accused of being misogynists. Both have enrolled in the military academy and invested in real estate. Both are backed by a foreign country.

Martelly won the 2011 Haiti election. The question is, Can Trump win the 2016 U.S. election?

The FBI leaks and the letter from James Comey have finally brought back home some top republicans who not only don't want to be blamed if Trump loses but also are concerned about the Supreme Court nomination.

FBI Director James Comey can be considered as a brilliant strategist. He upset some GOP leaders back in July for not recommending criminal charges against Hillary Clinton over her emails scandals.

He regained the Republicans' sympathy just a few days before the election by reopening the investigation, which gave Trump campaign a boost.

Less than 48 hours before election day, he makes the Democrats happy by clearing Hillary Clinton once again.

"Based on our review, we have not changed our conclusions that we expressed in July with respect to Secretary Clinton," he wrote in a letter to Congress on Sunday.

If the dramatic twist has lifted a cloud from Clinton campaign, it caused consternation in Trump camp. "...She's been protected by a rigged system...It's up to the American People to deliver justice at the ballot box on 8 November," Trump told supporters in Michigan on Sunday.

Comey's announcement that Hillary will face no charges in connection with newly discovered emails the bureau has been reviewing has a significant move in the stock market.

US stocks are spiking after declining for nine days in a row.

I predict a Trump loss will be chaos for the United States because not only Trump will contest the result of the election, his redneck supporters will break havoc toward the United States.

No matter the result, this election is one for the books.

SOURCES

The Populist Explosion John B. Judis

Whistle Stop John Dickenson

Second chance: Three Presidents and the Crisis of American Superpower Zbigniew Brzeziński

 Washington Post

 New York Times

The Wall Street Journal

United Nations Bulletin

The greatest show on earth, the deals, the down fall, the reinvention Wayne Barret

The Atlantic

USA today

Democracy in America Alexis de Tocqueville

The Origins of Totalitarianism Hannah Arendt

Politics Aristotle

The Future of Freedom: Illiberal Democracy at Home and Abroad Fareed Zakaria

The Tragedy of Great Power Politics John Mearsheimer

Why Nations Fail Daron Acemoglu and James A. Robinson

The Making of Modern Economics Mark Skousen

Is Our Children Learning Paul Begala

www.ingramcontent.com/pod-product-compliance
Lightning Source LLC
Chambersburg PA
CBHW022122280326
41933CB00007B/497